Sheringham Park

Norfolk

THE NATIONAL TRUST

Sheringham Park

Sheringham is the most complete and best preserved example of a park and house designed by the great landscape gardener Humphry Repton (1752–1818). Repton himself proclaimed it 'my most favourite work'. He was also keen on 'humanising, as well as animating, beautiful scenery' by allowing visitors into the park, and the National Trust's ownership of Sheringham has made this possible.

The Sheringham Landscape

When the retreating ice-sheet deposited its final, vast load of sand, shingle and clay across the north coast of Norfolk over 8,000 years ago, it provided the raw material for the landforms we see today. To the north of the Holt/Cromer ridge, which is made of this glacial debris, wooded, steep-sided valleys quickly give way to undulating farmland, pasture and sea cliffs. It is a landscape unlike any other found in the county and one which has stirred the human spirit for thousands of years. Natural forces and the labours of generations of farmers have shaped that landscape ever since.

In the late eighteenth century the owner of Sheringham, Cook Flower, created the framework for the present park by planting shelter belts of woodland on the more exposed hilltops. When Abbot Upcher took possession of the Sheringham estate on 10 July 1811, he was fully aware of the natural beauty of the place: 'What infinite variety presents itself in this enchanting spot ... Oh! What scenes of rational yet heartfelt pleasure do we not anticipate in the lovely Sheringham.' His choice of Repton to landscape the estate could not have been better.

The Temple; from Repton's Red Book

(*Above*) Humphry Repton's business card

(*Left*) Sheringham Cliffs

(*Far left*) Hall Farm stands near the site of Cook Flower's old house, which was replaced by Sheringham Hall

Repton and Sheringham

When Humphry Repton was first trying to establish himself as a landscape gardener in the 1780s, he had lived in the nearby village of Sustead, and must have known the area around Sheringham well. In 1809 he had suggested that the Sheringham estate would serve very well as the nation's gift to Admiral Nelson's family in honour of Norfolk's greatest seaman. Conveniently, Cook Flower was a client of Repton's son William, who was a solicitor in Aylsham, but neither father nor son managed to convince the Government. So William arranged to sell Sheringham to Abbot Upcher, having first cannily championed an Enclosure Bill which increased the value of the property. And when Upcher came to sign the contract (for £52,500) in July 1811, it was no coincidence that Humphry Repton should be visiting his son.

Abbot and Charlotte Upcher

The tragic early death of his elder brothers had made Abbot Upcher heir to his father's estate near Yarmouth at the tender age of twelve. In 1809 he married Charlotte Wilson, the daughter of the Rev. Henry Wilson of Kirby Cane near Geldeston in Norfolk. The couple shared a love of literature and were both deeply religious.

Soon after acquiring 'Sheringham Bower', as they called it, the Upchers commissioned Humphry Repton to remodel the landscape. Repton was then at the height of his powers and reputation, but, following a carriage accident in January 1811, was confined to a wheelchair. Nevertheless, he made no fewer than five visits to Sheringham in June 1812 to consult the Upchers. 'Frequent conversations on the spot with congenial minds' followed: 'I never forget that it is your happiness for which I am providing and with that in view I feel myself bounded by prudential limits as the property is by the sea.'

The Upchers regarded Flower's old farmhouse near Upper Sheringham village as unsuitable for their growing young family. So Repton turned to his architect son, John Adey Repton, to build them a new house in the Italian villa style of John Nash, in whose office John Adey had worked as an assistant.

(Left) Humphry Repton: 'After having passed nearly half a century in the study of Natural Scenery and having been professionally consulted in the improvement of many hundreds of places in different parts of England I can with truth pronounce, that Sheringham possesses more natural beauty and local advantages, than any place I have ever seen'

(Far left) Charlotte Upcher; by Richard Westall. Emma Upcher praised her mother's 'enthusiastic temperament, her exquisite enjoyment of existence in every shape, from the sublimest views to the simplest fern and wild flower, her glowing appreciation of all that was noble, talented or good'

Abbot Upcher; by George Henry Harlow. As his daughter Emma said of her parents: 'They found a spot they thought a Paradise, and there began to build their "bower"'

John Adey Repton's proposal for the new house from his father's Red Book

The Red Book

In July 1812 Repton presented his proposals in the form of one of his famous Red Books, so called because of their red morocco leather bindings. The text was written in a copperplate hand, and the book lavishly illustrated with watercolour views. Several of these make use of a paper 'slide', or flap, which allows one to see the same view before and after improvement. The text, typically, contains his comments on the site and its practicalities, and such poetry and prose as he thought might flatter his patron. The Red Book for Sheringham is of the large folio format which he reserved for his most prestigious commissions. He described Sheringham as his 'favourite and darling child in Norfolk'.

Park Lodge; from Repton's Red Book

Creating Sheringham Park

Within days of moving to Sheringham in October 1812, Abbot Upcher was laid low with a 'violent nervous fever' – a portent of greater tragedy to come. As a result, the planned improvements were slow to start.

In July 1813 the foundation stones of the Upchers' new house were laid – first, by their eldest son, Henry Ramey, then by Abbot, Charlotte, and their daughters, Mary and 'little Emma', who fell into the wet mortar. In 1815 the kitchen garden was laid out, and the Upper Approach, or main drive from the woods, made. Upcher considered this the 'greatest possible masterpiece of Repton's art in landscape gardening'. 1816 saw the planting of the woodlands, kitchen garden and orchards, and the first seeding of the parkland. Abbot recorded progress on the house in his journal, noting in November 1816 that the slaters had finished the roof.

The Upchers had hoped to move into their new house during the summer of 1817, but early in that year Abbot was again struck down with a fever. He left Sheringham with his family and was never to return, dying on 2 February 1819 at the age of only 35.

Sheringham Hall remained empty and unfinished for the next 20 years. Charlotte remained in Flower's old farmhouse, preferring to concentrate on managing the wider estate, and taking an active interest in the village and church, until her own death in 1857. The house was finally completed on a slightly more modest scale by her son, Henry Ramey Upcher, who moved in on his marriage in 1839.

The Upper Approach

The Repton Landscape

The Repton-designed Ivy Lodge (illustrated on p.1) at the main entrance to the estate marks the route of the Upper Approach to the house. This drive follows the crest of a natural ridge north through the woodland.

But as the slope at its extremity was too steep for horses to negotiate comfortably, the drive imperceptibly slips down off the ridge to the west and then turns sharply across its end. Repton took advantage of this practical consideration to stage-manage spectacular views of the sea, framed by woodland. The view to the right of the drive is obscured by the hillside and its dense planting until the edge of the park itself is reached. There, at the point known as 'The Turn', the first glimpse of the house 'will burst at once on the sight like some enchanted palace of a fairy tale'.

Repton admired the contorted shapes of the parkland trees, which had survived 'the brunt of many a storm'. He declared it to be 'dangerous for art to interfere', as removing the trees would expose those behind to a force they were unlikely to withstand. Instead, he considered them 'like a dry

'The view of the sea at Sheringham is not like that of the Bay of Naples.' With this wintery scene, Repton managed to persuade the Upchers against building their new house with a sea view

Before: the view north from 'The Turn', from Repton's Red Book

rugged channel of a winter's cataract, leaving in summer, sublime memorials of the power of Nature's mighty agents'.

The best site for the new house was hotly debated. The Upchers suggested that it should be close to 'The Turn' and face north in order to have views of the sea. Repton argued for a position in the lee of the Oak Wood with a south-facing aspect. A sea view might be pleasant in the Bay of Naples, but not in the harsh climate of the north Norfolk coast: '"Can it ever rain in Paradise?" In considering Sheringham as a permanent residence, and not as a mere summer villa, we must recollect how it may appear in winter.' Year-round considerations of light, shade and shelter also convinced Repton that the house should face slightly east of south to look squarely on to the main block of woodland. His view prevailed.

Repton's design for a garden temple, at a point now planted with trees, was not built. The present temple was erected in 1975 in a clearing left by dead elm trees slightly further north, and was opened on Thomas Upcher's seventieth birthday.

The view from the gazebo across the park to the Temple, which was built in 1975

After: the same view, showing the house carefully sheltered from the sea by Oak Wood Hill

The Later Upchers

Successive generations of Upchers continued to develop the estate broadly in accordance with the direction suggested by Repton in his Red Book.

Being so close to the sea in all its moods, the Upchers were only too aware of the dangers faced by those who made their living from it. The family's association with the Sheringham lifeboats has been a long one. They provided the rowed boats, the *Augusta* (named after Abbot and Charlotte's youngest daughter), and the *Henry Ramey Upcher*, which is preserved in Sheringham.

Henry Morris Upcher inherited the estate in 1892. He was an all-round sportsman, an excellent shot and a keen naturalist. As a member of an Icelandic expedition he discovered new information on the breeding ranges of Greylag Geese, and Upcher's Warbler was named in his honour by fellow naturalist Henry Tristram. At home he provided land and money for projects that turned the town of Lower Sheringham into a thriving centre of tourism. The golf course, promenade and sea defences were among the many schemes he supported.

Henry Morris was succeeded by Henry Edward Sparke (later Sir Henry) Upcher, who took his role as a farmer seriously. He inherited in the lean years after the First World War and farmed until the end of the Second World War. He served as chairman of the Norfolk Agricultural Executive Committee and required his own farm foreman to keep meticulous record of work and costs, but even if the corn was ripe and the weather set fair, none of his men was permitted to crank an engine or halter a horse on a Sunday.

Three years before Sir Henry's death in 1954, his son Thomas took over the running of the estate. Thomas had begun to take an interest in the estate some years earlier, and particularly in the rhododendron collection. He prevented many of the early introductions from being choked by the vigorous *Rhododendron ponticum*, which he said had to be 'restrained ruthlessly'. He also improved the diversity of the collection.

Thomas Upcher, who added to Sheringham's famous rhododendron collection. It was at his wish that the estate came to the National Trust in 1986

(*Left*) The Upchers paid for the Sheringham lifeboat, which was named after Henry Ramey Upcher

(*Far left*) Sir Henry Upcher

The Rhododendron Garden

The main approach drive to the house is flanked on both sides by approximately 20 hectares (50 acres) of rhododendrons. The date of the earliest plantings is thought to be around 1850. The garden has developed around a base planting of Scots pine and oak, with red-flowered forms of *Rhododendron arboreum* among the tallest of the rhododendrons and *Rhododendron ponticum* present in all its stages.

Early this century, seeds of various types were obtained by Henry Morris Upcher from the eminent plant-collector, Ernest 'Chinese' Wilson. Plants from this source include *Rhododendron ambiguum, calophytum* and *decorum*, among others.

After the Second World War, many more additions were made to the collection, which once had at least 65 species, and hundreds of named varieties. A great diversity of flower and leaf types gives additional interest, and several kinds flower outside the main season, for example the festive 'Christmas Cheer'.

Although there is much to see for those with a specialist interest in rhododendrons, it would be difficult to find anyone to whom the massed displays of hybrids at the end of May and in early June did not appeal. A planting of the red-flowered 'Britannia' covers part of one valley side, and the show of variously coloured azaleas midway along the drive is exceptionally beautiful, viewed between old sweet chestnut tree-trunks with tall rhododendrons behind and a ground layer of campion and bluebells in the foreground.

Many other species of tree and shrub are represented in the garden, including around fifteen kinds of magnolia alone, and the Pierises are believed to be among the largest in the country. Among the other trees are maples (*Acer*), Styrax, Eucryphia, the very popular Pocket Handkerchief Tree (*Davidia involucrata*) and a very big specimen of Snowdrop Tree (*Halesia*).

A rhododendron seedling involving the variety 'Mrs Furnivall'

A spectacular display of rhododendrons and azaleas in the woodland garden

The Rhododendron Drive seen through the trees in the woodland garden

Natural History

A male Smooth Newt

A male adder

The cliffs along the northern boundary of the estate form part of an important geological Site of Special Scientific Interest (SSSI), whose fossil beds have yielded up valuable information. The SSSI includes the cliff-top grassland, which was once both more extensive and richer in herbs.

Elsewhere, the woods are characterised by mixed-age plantings of Scots pine, beech, sweet chestnut and oak, including sessile oak, within remnants of ancient woodland and heath land. The acid soil serves to restrict the diversity of the flora, which is dominated by bracken and bramble over bluebells and climbing corydalis, with holly and rowan in the shrub layer. Nevertheless, several more unusual species can be found here, including wild service tree, wood sanicle and greater twayblade.

The parkland has been little cultivated, and old meadow grasses such as crested dogstail and quaking grass still occur, along with cowslip, bird's-foot trefoil and common spotted orchid.

Over 300 species of moths and nearly 30 species of butterfly have been recorded in the park in recent years. Insect life is encouraged both by leaving some dead timber lying where it falls, and by allowing the natural regeneration of woodland. Frogs, toads and smooth newts are commonly seen and, more rarely, the great crested newt. Like the newt, the adders at Sheringham are protected by law.

In addition to the many familiar resident and migrant breeding birds which may be seen here, less expected species are occasionally spotted on this important bird-watching coast.

Among the mammals, mice, voles and shrews are present in large numbers, as well as moles, hedgehogs, hares, foxes and three species of deer – roe, red and muntjac. Several species of bat, including long-eared and noctule bats, have roosts in the woods.

Occasionally, marine mammals are spotted from the cliff-top, such as common porpoises and seals.

A Great Spotted Woodpecker

The cliffs at Sheringham

The National Trust

Mildred Cordeaux; by Edward Halliday, 1968. A fluent Swedish speaker, she had an exciting career, working first for MI5 before transferring to MI6 during the Second World War. By her will she provided a munificent endowment for Sheringham, and the Trust owes this very significant benefactor and friend a special debt of gratitude

Having no heir, Thomas Upcher was anxious that the estate should be preserved, and it was his wish that the National Trust should become the guardian of Sheringham Park, for the benefit of the nation. This came about in 1986 thanks to bequests from E.L. Elliot, H. Ridler, D.E. Swiffen and Alice M. Weeks, grant-aid from the National Heritage Memorial Fund, the Countryside Commission and the Nature Conservancy Council, and funds raised by the East Anglia Coast & Countryside Appeal.

The late Mildred Cordeaux, née Upcher, a cousin of Thomas Upcher, knew Sheringham all her life and played a leading role in its acquisition by the Trust. As a young girl, she used to like climbing the gazebo on the top of Oak Wood. Recognising that its restoration would not be a priority for the Trust, she very generously paid for a replacement, which was lifted into position by an RAF Sea King helicopter four days after the Great Storm of 15–16 October 1987. It was officially opened by the Prince of Wales on 20 January 1988.

Weybourne Heath was purchased in 1994 with grants from the Countryside Commission, North Norfolk District Council and the Woods bequest. The Heath is subject to a lease to Forest Enterprise and is managed jointly with the National Trust. Recently, Sheringham has also benefited from a substantial legacy from Mr and Mrs S.W. Smith.

The new gazebo was erected on Oak Wood Hill in 1987 on the site of a look-out post built during the Napoleonic Wars